Monarch

Monarch

written by Michael S Canter

from a collection of bedtime stories for the Canter Kids

Monarch

It is his nursery, larder and very curiously, his one defense

It was the milkweed in the yard that failed. There were only two plants, left there by the gardener for the butterflies, and one had become infested with gold aphids. It died outright in three days time. Caterpillars on the weed had to find a new place to live and there just wasn't one.

The common milkweed has evolved over time to be host to several types of insects, but principally to the Monarch Butterfly. This summer charmer is a delight to the eye and milkweed is the only home he has. It is his nursery, larder and very curiously, his one defense in a very dangerous place: your back yard!

Snakes, spiders, ants, birds and frogs; all would love to sink a fang into a fat juicy caterpillar or into a flapping, nectar sipping adult butterfly. Why do they not? I can tell you the answer in a single word. Poison!

The milkweed (and its' milky looking sap) is deadly poison to every creature on earth except the Monarch Butterfly. As a tiny but voracious caterpillar, he eats and eats and grows and grows, devouring leaf after leaf of lethal salad, storing death in every cell, yet is unharmed by the cruel toxin within. They might look like candy on wings to us but all the predators in all your back yards know, by their colors, "Don't eat Monarchs"!

Safe then from claw and tooth, they eat milkweed leaves and wait till suddenly, something happens. The tilt of the sun, a message from ancestors coded in the weed or maybe just the end of gluttony demands a change, right now! The bloated sodden worm wraps himself in emerald blanket, hangs it from a leaf and closes the top with brass latches and buttons.

Inside there is no eat nor sun nor drink. We cannot see in, he cannot see out. Yet something is happening, something amazing that no human has ever seen.

Do you believe in miracles?

II.
They are not food, yet they are fragile and there is chance. There is fire and frost and aphids to kill the weed. When the change came, the caterpillar had no place to go. In desperation, he sought another weed but could find none. He crawled across a concrete driveway, then up a garage door, looking frantically for the leaf that would sustain him. When it happened, he was nowhere near a leaf; the change was now, now NOW!

Completely out of choices, he plastered himself to a rectangular panel of the garage door, all at wrong angles, not straight but stuck like bird poop to the side of the wooden house. Sometimes there just isn't any more time.

III.
If you went to see the magic show, you might be delighted to see the magician pull a rabbit from his hat and you would certainly be astonished to see a woman sawed in two before your very eyes. If the magician said though, "Hey kid, you want to see me change a caterpillar into a beautiful butterfly?" maybe you would head for the exit, regretting the money you had wasted on the cheap "magic show". Do we look like rubes? Certainly no magician could perform a trick like that!

Visit www.monarch-butterfly.com/ to see more

IV.

The girl awoke in her bed with a sense of alarm. Something was wrong! She couldn't feel her arm! She tried to bring her hand to her face but it would not obey her. She rolled over in a panic and there it was; still attached but unresponsive and numb- of course she had just slept on it so long that normal circulation had been interrupted and her momentary panic vanished as feeling crept back into the recalcitrant limb. Still, as she stood before the mirror, combing her long hair with the other hand, the wrong hand, what would happen if one day her arm did not return to normal? She wondered, indeed marveled, at the prospect of having always to use her other hand her entire life.

V.

We remember little of what came before. Of a sudden, we have huge compound eyes, the world flashes around us. Our powerful muscles strain and burst our bonds. Sleek chitin armor glistens in the morning sun as our new limbs grasp and tackle the ragged edges of the chrysalis and cast it aside. We have air and sunlight, a new set of chances and needs. We are so powerful!

VI.

The front wing on the right side was folded like bad origami, a neat straight crease that stopped the wing from ever opening and stiffening for flight. The improper attachment to the garage door had prevented the right side of the chrysalis from developing correctly. No matter how the Monarch flexed and pumped his wings for flight, he would not accompany his tribe to far away Michoacán. The migration must proceed without him-

VII.

After school the girl walked up her rainy driveway. She saw the black and orange butterfly lying on the cold concrete. She got her brother from inside the house and together they scooped him into a jar. Her dad had told her, indeed warned her, not to get involved with wild animals of any kind. You can't help them and your best intentioned efforts will only serve to frighten the creature and hurt him further. Don't do it! "Nature takes care of its own", he said.

Her dad (whom she really did respect and trust) wasn't home yet though so she got her brother to smuggle in the jar, just so they could get a better look at the wretched rumpled Lepidoptera. Maybe when he dried out and got his bearings he would be okay again.

This wasn't the same thing her dad was talking about anyway.

This wasn't really trying to help a wild animal, at least not the way her dad had meant. It was hurt and needed to be, not helped, but just rescued for a little while. So she put a stick in the jar for the Monarch to climb on, then filled a bottle cap with sugar water and a drop of pear juice so he could have a drink.

Photo courtesy of Idaho Fish and Game

http://hemidatlanticlounge.com/2014/04/28/the-swallows-of-san-juan-capistrano/

VIII.

The Lord of The Migration has a great influence over many god's creatures. Fish, fowl and great herd beasts all bow to him. Atlantic salmon, Canada geese and American bison are in his thrall. When he speaks, "go a thousand miles", they go. "Go to fire, go to flood", they go. "Go, even if you are frightened or sick or hungry, even if there is a wolf", they go.

He is a horrid squat bully, stinking and unwashed, without friends of any sort. He has no parents. He wonders how and why he became a king but has no answer. In all the spirit world, no one speaks to him.

Finally though, his subjects do very well. At the end of the migration is green grass and flowers and pretty waterfalls. Sprites fly over with bowls of nectar and plaster balm for their scratches..Eggs hatch and babes drink their mothers milk. They do not hate the lord of the migration but neither do they thank him. There was ever only one fear-being left behind.

Monarch butterflies fill the sky. Photo by Ann Ryan/Monarch Watch.

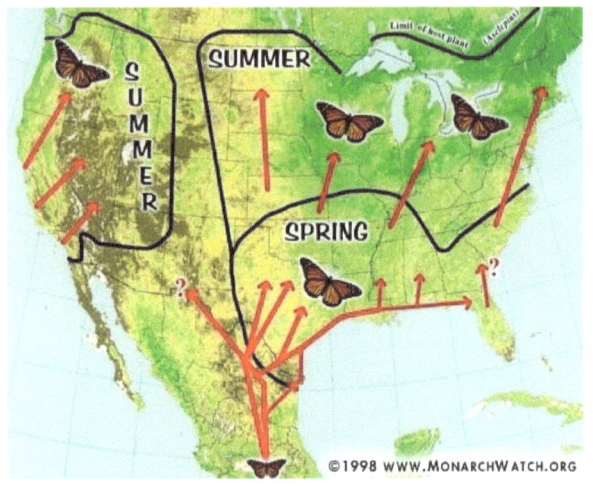

IX.
Monarch butterflies in North America are of two houses. By far, the largest is that east of the Rocky Mountains. They range from the Pacific coast of central Mexico to summers reach in northern Ontario. They flip and flap and seem at leisure but they are pushed relentlessly to travel north and visit every milkweed. And when the tilt of the planet aims away from the big star, they spin on their heels and turn around, envisioning a soft and lovely Michoacan, where it never snows.

The western tribe of Mariposa Monarca has a much easier time of it. Their summer holiday takes them into the highlands of the great mountains. Like the eastern group however, they cannot cross to the other side. Their adventure takes them no further than the tree line, then they turn around.

They still must contend with the change of seasons, of course, and cities, highways and farms and lawns where every last Milkweed is pulled, poisoned and burned out of existence. They somehow manage though with a little help from their friends who might leave a few growing in a corner of the yard or in a ditch. At the end of the Western Monarchs migration, they settle and rest in trees, thousands of them together, in the beautiful seaside town of Santa Cruz, California.

"You're gonna get in trouble," it was the boy speaking. The girl, younger by three years, didn't look at him; just stared into the thick glass jar and its' prisoner. The jar had no lid; none was needed. The Monarch with the folded wing would not fly out and his perch did not reach the top of the glass.

She thought of a name for the caged creature, then quickly discarded it. Nicknames had become popular in her school lately and she had been given an unpleasant one, so she had already decided never to use them.

"Dad's not gonna like this," the boy was starting to enjoy baiting her.

"Oh, please, just stop it!" she snapped. "Dad's not going to care at all! It's just a bug in a jar!"

Taken aback by her vehemence, the boy scrambled from the room and wandered off in search of other amusement.

Indeed, she surprised herself when she spoke sharply to her brother and more so that the remark had it's desired effect. He was gone, chased away, not in her face, removed and no longer a factor. She made a mental note.

Quieting, she cradled the jar in her lap, warming the glass against her body. A sense of orange and black ebbed through and she imagined a clanked face, eyes that see into the heart of another world, a coiled proboscis for the exquisite liquor of flowers. She heard her mother say, "Just a small one for me, thanks". The ring of one crystal glass touching another.

Her wings flapped once and the lift astonished her. There was only a slight effort then her flailing arms and legs shifted shape and balance, then locked on the air. For a moment she forgot who she was. For a moment, it seemed she was being held.

She felt sunlight warming her wings and face, such a vast reach of strength and power. Without trying, she saw others like herself, many hundreds, on a road of air and light. She did not follow though she knew this would be her only chance.

The vision was gone in an instant, the offer withdrawn and her room fell back into shape around her. She placed the jar on her shelf and stood in the center of the carpet. She positioned her left foot and moved her right foot only. Stepping in a circle, arms extended for balance and the memory of flight- It just felt better than being still. Her hair was undone and she felt sick. Thumping the circle dance, she went round and round.

The boy came crashing back into the room, pulling his father by the hand. The man was puzzled and sort of amused to be included in a kids dilemma, a problem so serious they would call in the adults for help. It wasn't something he was good at; he'd forgotten almost everything he had known as a kid. When he saw the girl though, he was shocked. Her face was marked with tears and had a look of genuine anger. She looked at her dad like she didn't know who he was.

He took her hands in his own as if they were to dance, but it was just to stop her spinning and stamping her foot in that painful way. He recalled a line from a story he had heard when he was his daughter's age, the only story his father had ever read to him and he asked it now, "Why are you crying?"

XI

Next day she was okay again. It was Saturday so she was home hanging out with her brother. Her dad had tidied up and made pancakes. Her brother was kicking a ball against the garage and yelling at it. He now imagined himself the protector of little sisters everywhere. She watched her mother carefully as she brought a china cup to her lip and sipped hot tea. The woman soon became aware she was being studied, said, "Would you like some tea?"

"They give us back so much more than we can possibly give them." The woman on the radio was talking about dogs, pets in our homes-but now the girl thought about people she had heard about. A man bitten by a wolf; an animal he had struck with his car and stopped to help. An old woman on a beach pouring pails of seawater over the sunburnt skin of a dying whale. She had seen college students at great oil spills trying to wash petroleum from the wings of sea birds. On the surface, they looked like fools. Those animals couldn't be saved. Yet they all had one thing in common as they worked on individual beasts; they had all very recently been crying but now they were not. She wondered if they understood these animals are dying, you can't save them; you can only frighten them and hurt them further! My dad said so!

XII

The jar was peaceful and the view from inside was curved and beautiful. Light from glowing bulbs followed the shape of the glass. He could see the girl and her family moving in the larger room and he crawled up his perch to join them but, alas, it did not reach the top.

The Monarch delighted to hang upside down from his perch; to climb the several branches and touch the wall of his universe with his front feet, tap tap; could they hear it? The touch of his front claw against the smooth hard surface, tap, tap?

Like most creatures, his strongest sense was olfactory. His food dish on the floor of his jar was too odiferous and the girl who brought it with a smile was a wonderful smell. He sent his own pheromones into the air, a rich and complex love letter to her but he couldn't tell if she understood it or not. It seemed she didn't but sometimes he believed she did. He couldn't be sure.

His favorite smell though was the brewing of tea. The feel and sense of steam would come on the air and he learned what came next. The clink and ring of china and a shared silver spoon and the scrape of a chair moved across the floor. The tip of the spoon crunched into the dried tea leaves. The smell bespoke all the wild gardens from Canada to Mexico.

XIII

The woman brought down two tea cups, so thin that light shone through them, painted by an artist long gone to her reward. She sat a saucer and cup on the table in front of her daughter and the same set on her side. She placed the pot between them. When the kettle blew clouds of steam into the air she turned off the fire and brought the kettle to the pot. She poured 'till the pot was nearly full and returned the kettle to the stovetop. Honey, napkins and a plate of shortbread completed the setting. She sat down.

After a moment the tea was steeped and ready. The woman filled her cup first, then the girls. She stirred honey in then passed the spoon to the girl. She did exactly as her mother had done then laid down the spoon. Both sat breathing in the perfume of the tea, turning the cup that was so like a flower to bring it's handle to the tips of their fingers.

They were unaware how the bouquet of Ceylon tea filled the room and was shared by the exotic insect in the thick glass jar. They sat straight, did not put their elbows on the table, and after each sip, returned the cup to it's saucer.

The woman slid the plate of shortbread toward the girl who took one and placed it on the saucer next to the cup.

Each contemplated the other. The child hid her amazement how beautiful her mother suddenly seemed. She watched as the porcelain flower trembled at her mothers' lip, then came away. Her breath mixed with the breath of the cup. Her long graceful fingers supported the tiny creation from every side. She thought again of the butterfly and the perfection of its' shiny black claws; the coiled mouth parts like the spring of a wind-up clock on your grandfather's mantle. The woman hid her amazement too, how beautiful her daughter suddenly seemed.

XIV

Next day, the sun-up, the girl walked to the edge of her yard where shrubs started again. She laid the jar on it's side under the shelter of a copper beech. It looked like a little glass house, half in sunlight, half in shade. She said goodbye to the Monarch and walked away.

Milkweed Life Cycle

July 2017 a Monarch arrives in Michigan and feeds on Hydrangea blossoms before depositing eggs for its 3rd generation in this year's migration journey.

Our Monarch joins the pupa party on milkweed in West Michigan to lay eggs

Monarch caterpillars enjoy feasting on milkweed leaves.

The 3rd generation Monarch butterflies that hatch in Michigan will fly to Canada, and lay the eggs that produce the 4th generation migrating to Mexico for the winter.

Monarch caterpillars attach to an overhanging surface and their chrysalis with its golden crown is suspended during the transformation

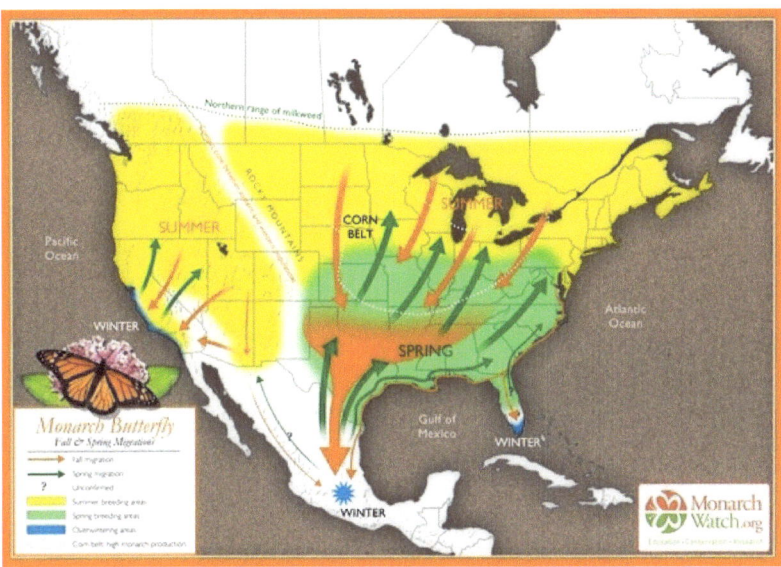

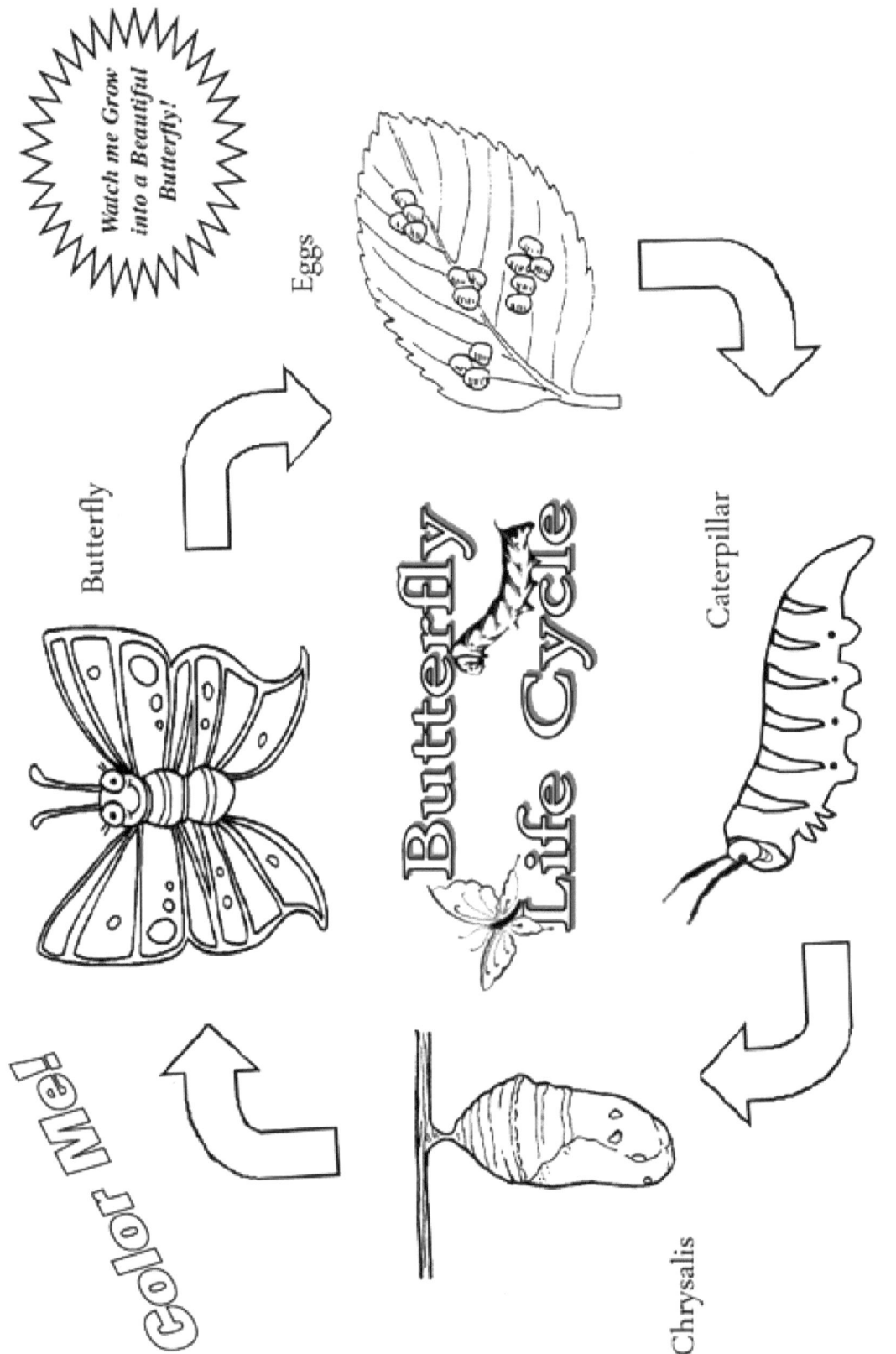

Watch me Grow into a Beautiful Butterfly!

Eggs

Butterfly

Butterfly Life Cycle

Caterpillar

Color Me!

Chrysalis

Want more cool critters? Please visit www.NatureGifts.com for other complete live kits containing all sorts of fascinating critters.

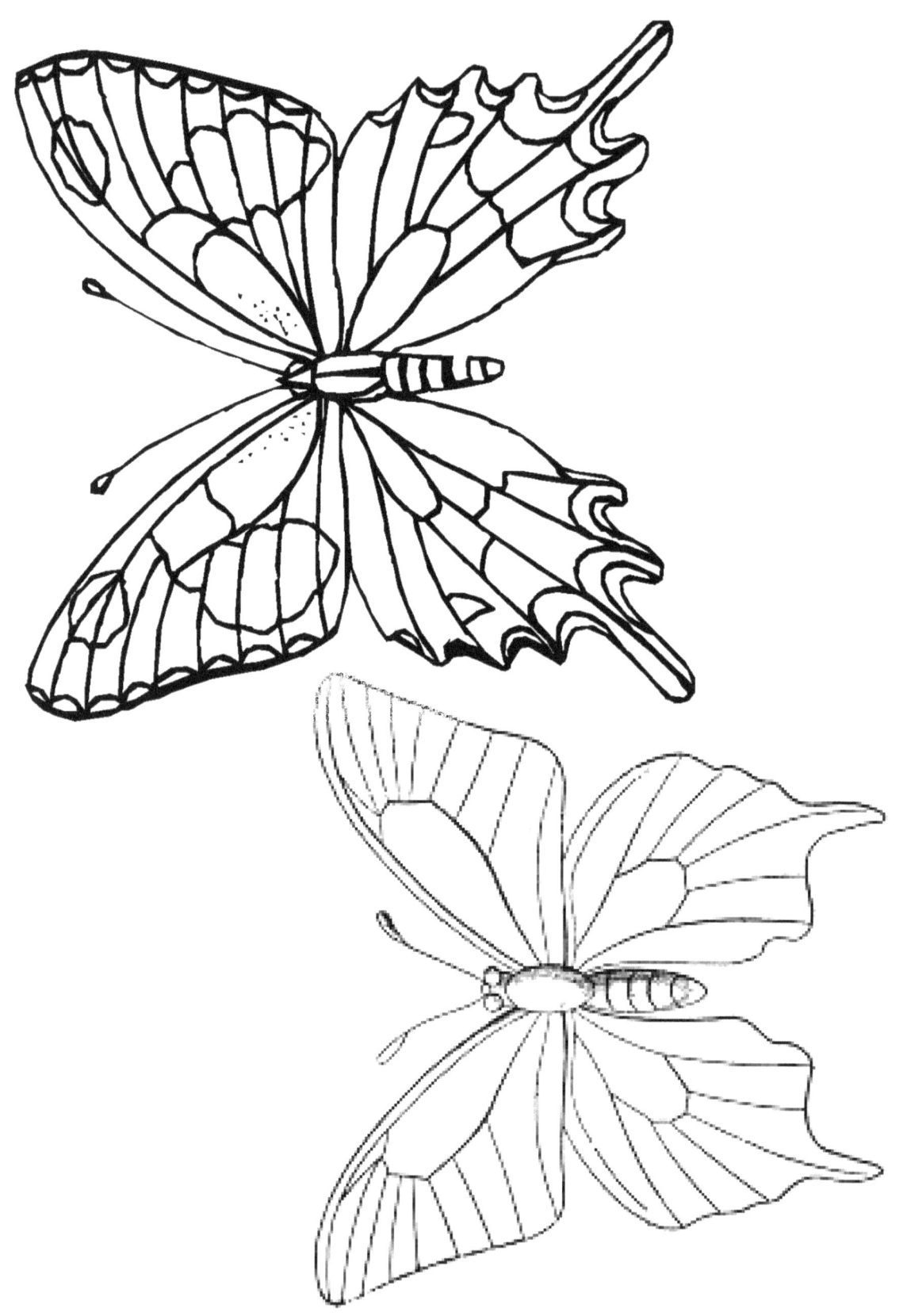